# TENNIS TENETS

## *Wit and Wisdom*
## *On and Off the Court*

**Eggman Publishing Company**
**Nashville, Tennessee**

ISBN: 1-886371-34-2

## ORDERING INFORMATION

To order copies of *Tennis TeNets* please send a check for $7.95 (includes shipping & handling) per copy to:

***Tennis Matters!***
**P. O. Box 382834**
**Germantown, TN  38183-2834**

Call for quantity discounts:  901-737-0001

# Acknowledgments

The author acknowledges a deep debt of gratitude owed to many persons who have helped with this work. Most of all, my hearty thanks go to daughters Barbara and Wendy and my long-suffering wife Tommie. They have made immeasurable contributions. *Tennis TeNets* would not have been completed without their help.

Special thanks go to tennis pros Jim Shackelford, Cindy Davis and Jim Swiggart and neighbors Beverly and Hank Bruninga who helped with editing. Many of my fellow hackers and tennis friends have contributed either knowingly or unknowingly. I hope they'll recognize their contributions and feel warmly thanked.

My deepest appreciation goes to all of these folks. They made significant contributions to whatever success the book may achieve. I alone am responsible for its shortcomings.

# INTRODUCTION

*Tennis TeNets* was inspired by a lifelong interest in tennis and by exemplary tennis stars, including Arthur Ashe, Billie Jean King, Rod Laver, Jimmy Connors, Chris Evert, Martina Navratilova, John McEnroe and many others.

As an avid tennis hacker and lover of the game for many years, I play and watch tennis at every opportunity. I began to develop items for *Tennis TeNets* during TV coverage of the Grand Slam Events of 1993. Having recently read *Life's Little Instruction Book* by H. Jackson Brown and being deeply moved by the untimely and tragic death of Arthur Ashe, I undertook to write an LLIB for those who love and play the game.

# To the Reader

Tenets are principles, opinions or beliefs commonly held as true. Tennis tenets, or *TeNets*, as used in this book, include some of the common lore and common sense of the great game of tennis and its relationship to the great game of life. Tennis TeNets are selected to make you think about these challenging games.

I have attempted to include some tennis humor. For years, and with little success, I have looked for original tennis humor. What little I've found has often been borrowed or converted from golf humor, of which there seems to be a limitless supply. I have been unable to find an explanation for this other than that tennis is no joke.

I hope you enjoy and benefit from *Tennis TeNets* and that the book's wit and wisdom will entertain and benefit you on and off the court.

# TeNets

Following are some of the TeNets guiding the development and selection of the more than 500 tips, quips and quotes included in the book:

• Tennis provides opportunities for putting into practice lessons about life learned at home, in school, in church and in other activities of daily living.

• Playing tennis prolongs youth and promotes good health.

• Laughter is a part of most every tennis occasion. Players learn to laugh at themselves and with each other in the fun-and-games attitude that usually prevails on and off court.

• Players who play their personal best and abide by the rules find tennis a source of recreation and renewal.

• The practice involved in improving one's tennis game helps develop the patience and persistence important for success both in tennis and in life.

• Players should know and understand the rules, but more than that, they must apply them in the light of good judgment, established custom and longstanding tradition.

• Rudeness and gamesmanship have no place in the game as it should be played.

• Tennis creates opportunities for learning the give-and-take and good sportmanship admired in successful people.

• Among the secrets of a long and happy life is the kind of lifelong learning that can be found in the sport for a lifetime, tennis.

• For those who love and play the game, the unique enjoyment to be found in tennis is among life's greatest pleasures.

• Tennis provides opportunities for sharing and socializing, for making new friends and enhancing relationships with old friends.

• Interest in tennis must be kept in perspective and not indulged at the expense of the other important aspects of life and daily living.

# A Little History

The earliest origins of tennis are probably to be found in a handball game of ancient Greece. It was called *sphairistike.* As early as the 1400s, France originated a related game played in the courts of royalty and thus known as court tennis or royal tennis, a game still played today.

The modern game of tennis, much like the one we now play, was invented by Major Walter C. Wingfield of Great Britain. He packaged and patented the game in 1874, and it was brought to the U.S. soon after. Early tennis tournaments were played in England at various sites including Wimbledon and in the U.S. in the late 1870s. The U.S. Lawn Tennis Association was formed in 1881. Davis Cup Competition began in 1900. The first U.S. Open Tournament was held in 1920, the first for women in 1936. The National Lawn Tennis Hall of Fame was established in 1955 at Newport, Rhode Island.

The game itself, as invented by Major Wingfield, has remained much the same over the years except for the introduction of the tie-break. Extensive improvements have been made in equipment, in the numbers and caliber of players, and in their strength and physical fitness.

In the past forty years, worldwide interest in tennis has grown due to visibility of the game through television and the building of elaborate venues for play at Grand Slam Tournament sites in Australia, France, England, and the U.S. Interest has also been stimulated by Davis Cup international competition, by such groups as the U.S. Tennis Association, and by great players competing for huge sums of prize money. These factors have stimulated widespread participation by individuals at the local level, and this interest will continue to grow as we approach the 21st century.

An excellent history and the most comprehensive source of information about tennis is the *Encyclopedia of Tennis* published in 1994, by Bud Collins, a great reporter and popularizer of the game for more than forty years.

*Tennis TeNets* was published in 1996 and the rest, as they say, will be history.

1. Isn't it great that every tennis game starts with the score love-all?

2. The time for tennis is anytime. Tennis time is a state of mind, not a clock hour.

3. The greatest tennis match of all time was played one point at a time.

4. Losing a point because your shot is barely caught by the net cord seems wholly unfair and unjustified.

5. Enter tournaments; they're fun and great experience.

6. Increase your chances of winning points by making your opponents run and reach to return shots.

7. Though not stated explicitly in the rules of tennis, you should give the benefit of the doubt to your opponent when you are uncertain of the proper line call.

8. Get to know the feel of your strokes by practicing them in slow motion.

9. Play tennis and have a ball.

10. An ace in time may save a game!

11. The basic warm-up and flexibility exercises include *knee-chest flex, spinal twist* and stretches of the *hamstrings, quadriceps, shoulders, groin, calf, hips* and *forearms.* They're well worth doing to avoid injury.

12. Early racquet preparation is essential to the success of every tennis stroke.

13. Tennis fantasies are all in your mind!

14. The sweet spot in tennis is any court on which you win. The sweet spot on a racquet includes the frame and handle if you've hit a winner.

15. There are no traps, bunkers or water-holes on a tennis court, but there are bad bounces, poor line calls and of course the @#$%&*!! net.

16. Fun tennis is a service (especially an ace) to a friend.

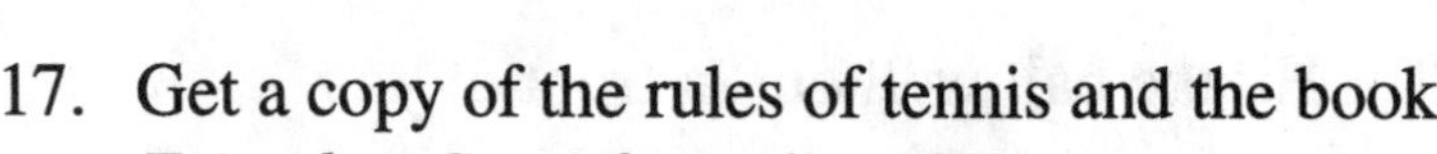

17. Get a copy of the rules of tennis and the book *Friend at Court* from the USTA.

18. The most crucial point in a tennis game is either the previous one or the next one, but you have to win the last one to win the game, set, match or championship.

19. Tennis vocabulary is very sophisticated–lob, dink, drop-shot, fault, "oh no!" and "yours!" Some is unprintable.

20. Hit the ball well out in front of you.

21. Read the spin and pace of the ball as it comes from the face of the opponent's racquet so you will know where and how it will bounce. Hearing and interpreting the sound of the impact will also help.

22. Every tennis court is 78 feet long. Your half is 39 feet long. Cover it well.

23. Don't let the impulse to be cute ruin your drop-shot, put-away or smash.

24. Weekend tennis may include a series of Sunday or Sabbath morning services.

25. Don't touch the net during a point or you lose it (the point, that is).

26. A ball that's going out is well left.

27. Stick to a winning game; change a losing game.

28. Join a group at or above your level of play. Aspire to be better.

## Tennis TeNets Top Ten Tips–Number 1

WATCH THE BALL. Keeping your eyes on the ball is essential to good eye-hand coordination. Focusing on the ball helps you read its direction, spin and pace as it comes from the opponent's racquet. Follow the ball all the way to the face of your racquet to make a good shot. "Keep your eye on the ball" is among the most often repeated advice in tennis.

29. Be Ashe(n)–don't let them know how you really feel when you're down or angry. Be Arthurian, have good court manners.

30. Play with weaker players to help them develop their games. Remember when you were one.

31. Adopt a grip-style best suited to you, such as the shake-hands-with-the-racquet grip.

32. Visualize and anticipate success. Expect the breaks to go your way.

33. Shower luxuriously and therapeutically.

34. Hope springs eternal in tennis players.

35. A good guideline is to play a third of the time with better players, a third with equal players and a third with weaker opponents.

36. Pause, take a deep breath and relax before the big points!

37. Good service means no double faults.

38. The singles court is 27 feet wide. Guard it well.

39. Change something when you're losing, especially your frame of mind.

40. Use compliments such as "good shot," "great shot," "good get," "well-played," "wow" and "well-done." Mumble under your breath when saying "what luck" or "s/he's not *that* good."

41. Surprise, the opponent's surprise, that is, is a key to good drop shots.

42. Older players can show you a few new wrinkles.

43. On a sleepless night, don't count sheep; relive your good shot(s).

44. Have a prematch ritual that includes a careful stretch and warm-up to compose yourself. Include plans to do your personal best.

45. Nothing beats an ice bag, aspirin, your favorite cool drink and a win to help cure minor injuries.

46. The deuce court is on your right as you face the net; the ad (advantage) court is on the left. Some call them the forehand and backhand respectively, but this only applies to right-handed players.

47. Widen your circle of tennis friends. Introduce them to other players you know.

48. When preparing for your match, focus on good form and previous successes.

49. Should you happen to be playing with a partner named Brutus who has double-faulted while serving to formidable opponents, you may want to quote Shakespeare. "The fault, dear Brutus, is not in our stars, but in ourselves, that we are underlings."

50. Concentrate! Loss of concentration can lead to unforced errors.

51. The ball that barely trickles over the net in your favor seems like your just desserts.

## Tennis TeNets Top Ten Tips–Number 2

BEND YOUR KNEES. Bending your knees helps you maintain balance and be ready to move in any direction. When you're in a relaxed crouch with your knees bent, you can move toward the ball quickly to hit with accuracy and power. A popular tennis advice book is titled *Watch the Ball, Bend Your Knees, That'll Be Twenty Dollars, Please.*

52. U. S. Tennis Association Rule 2 says tennis officials (umpires, referees, net-cord judges and lines persons) are included among the permanent fixtures of the court.

53. Stand still and be quiet when watching a tennis court in play–it may be a critical point.

54. Take practice serves before play–none of that "first-one-in" to start a game.

55. Don't underestimate the power of positive thinking!

56. Forget the missed previous point–don't let it affect the next.

57. Tennis is a metaphor for life, for love, for war.

58. A ball 99% out is 100% good!

59. Join the United States Tennis Association and/or the American Tennis Association and read their magazines.

60. Enjoy those *free* points when your second serves are aces or draw unforced errors.

61. Watch good tennis whenever possible.

62. Effective footwork is essential to good tennis.

63. Let an instructor help you break bad habits by substituting better ones.

64. Prepare for a good ground stroke by rotating your body.

65. Don't choke. Don't even think about choking. Press on!

66. Pick a good player as a model and practice good form like that of the pros you admire.

67. Take a day off from tennis.

68. Remember, a bad day at court is better than no tennis at all, even for lawyers.

69. Move your feet. Never stand still.

70. Don't lose a friend over tennis.

71. "Move forward!" is advice that cannot be repeated too often. Move forward.

72. Tennis requires mental toughness. Mental toughness means keeping your composure when things go wrong. It means continuing to do your best even when things look grim.

73. Wrong-foot your opponent every chance you get. It's tiring and frustrating to be wrong-footed.

74. Tennis players are hard to match.

*Think About It*

## Press On

Nothing in the world can take the place of persistence.

Talent will not; nothing is more common than unsuccessful men with talent.

Genius will not; unrewarded genius is almost a proverb.

Education alone will not; the world is full of educated derelicts.

Persistence and determination alone are omnipotent.

*—Calvin Coolidge*

75. Think how much more fun tennis is than golf!

76. Encourage others, especially family members, to learn to play tennis.

77. Revel in the fact you can play tennis your whole life long. Katherine Hepburn played two-bounce tennis in her 80s.

78. Good tennis is a total experience in which you are fully immersed.

79. For each match, adopt a strategy and a set of tactics designed to help you win.

80. Keep your opponent back near the baseline–don't give up short balls.

81. Toss high (but not too high) for a good serve.

82. Take the net whenever you can.

83. Those who hesitate lose.

84. Serve deep, right near the corners and at the “T.”

85. Sponsor a child for tennis camp.

86. Good tennis playing posture looks strange any place other than on court.

87. Welcome back, Monica!

88. Keep the pressure on your opponent.

89. Tennis is a game that requires self-discipline. Don’t let yourself get out of hand.

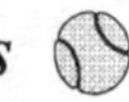

90. Don't carry a grudge into a tennis match.

91. Keep your body language positive no matter how discouraged or tired you feel.

92. Help senior citizens continue playing.

93. On taking the court, you're assumed to be fit. Don't blame losses or mistakes on unfitness.

94. Learn to juggle while you wait. The balls are handy.

95. Leave the court in better shape than you found it.

96. A day without tennis is like a day without spice in your life.

97. Age and cunning beat youth and running.

98. Have you ever seen any behavior so variable as styles of serving?

99. If you can't play regular tennis, play from a wheelchair or play short-court, two-bounce or some adapted form with someone with similar capabilities.

**Tennis TeNets Top Ten Tips–Number 3**

ANTICIPATE, PREPARE. Think ahead so you can visualize and realize success. Develop points with a series of shots rather than trying to win each with a single stroke. Anticipate where the ball is going so you can get your racquet back early for a crisp volley, firm ground stroke, strong smash, top-spin lob or well-placed drop shot. Prepare for success.

100. Patronize your pro's shop for restringing, grip renewal, new equipment and/or a friendly chat.

101. Yannick Noah's excellent lob was known as "Noah's arc."

102. Look your opponents in the eye, but don't stare them down.

103. Tennis is a multisensory game. Vision, hearing, touch and the kinesthetic sense are all important. Taste, except for attire, isn't too critical.

104. Be sure you have arrangements for your next match before you leave today's.

105. It's forgivable to play tennis as you enjoy it, including ignoring the advice of experts!

106. An unwritten rule of tennis is that players must call unobserved rule infractions on themselves. Examples are balls that bounce twice or almost imperceptibly tick the racquet, hair, clothing or body.

107. With current exotic materials, computer technology and modern marketing practices, today's racquet is tomorrow's heirloom and next season's archeological find.

108. Tennis cannot be taken too seriously!

109. Enjoy the sound of a winning shot coming from your racquet.

110. Tennis is a good racquet.

111. A good ratio of aces to double faults is 3:1 or 4:1.

112. What Pogo said is especially true of tennis, "We have met the enemy and he is us!" It's true because the greatest problem for most tennis players is unforced errors–the ones we cause ourselves to make.

113. If you can win key points you can win the match, even if you win fewer than half of the total points.

*Think About It*

In losing a tennis point, game or match, one goes through a grief process (Elisabeth Kübler Ross) much like that of those who lose a loved one:

*Denial*–I can't believe it!!
*Anger*–@#$%*™£¢!
*Depression*–Woe is me.
*Bargaining*–If you'll just let me. . .
*Acceptance*–Aw well, that's life; it's only a game; let's get on with it.

114. You don't have to be a racketeer to play tennis, but you do have to go to court!

115. In singles, you have 1,053 square feet of court to cover. High lobs make that many more cubic feet to handle!

116. Help underprivileged children learn to play–share your retired equipment.

117. Increase your tennis attention span. Don't try to end points too quickly.

118. Your serve must land in an area 13.5 x 21 feet. Hmmm–pros do it at 100 or more mph!

119. Don't take golf too seriously.

120. Think through your opponent's weaknesses; then exploit them.

121. Have a treat and/or fellowship after the game.

122. Change partners occasionally.

123. Know your tennis strengths and use them!

124. Play tennis any day, not only on weekends and holidays.

125. Think of tennis as a focus for friendship, too.

126. Play mixed doubles and singles!

127. Hit through the ball and follow through!

128. It's timing that gives power to good tennis shots.

129. Be modest in victory; compliment losing opponents.

## Tennis TeNets Top Ten Tips–Number 4

ROTATE YOUR BODY. Most tennis strokes and serves start with the side of the player's body toward the net. Hold your body to the side and lean into your shot so you can hit through the ball with accuracy and power. Visualize the way baseball batters stand at bat and golfers rotate their bodies in hitting the ball.

130. Don't glare or mumble at the opponent(s) for what you think is a bad call.

131. A great ace is a service, not a bandage.

132. Adjust your attitude to playing conditions and opponents.

133. Move your feet on every point. You should be going where you expect the ball to be.

134. Don't interrupt play to towel off, change equipment or hold a conversation.

135. U. S. Tennis Association Rule 10 says it is a fault if you miss the ball (whiff) when serving.

136. With tennis, as with eggs, it's sometimes better to poach!

137. Have a rulebook and net-height gauge in your equipment bag, but don't be the court lawyer.

138. It is very difficult to hit a good shot while you are retreating.

139. Know CPR in case a player needs assistance. It would be good if the venue where you play has first aid and oxygen equipment.

140. Don't gamble on tennis.

141. Hit a defensive shot, a lob for example, to cope with a difficult point.

142. The child's riddle, "What's served but never eaten?" doesn't take into account the overhead smash at the opposing player.

143. Reward yourself immediately with a silent comment or gesture for every good shot.

144. Time is measured in milliseconds on the tennis court. Make split-second timing work for you.

145. Be nice to golfers. They have handicaps and deal with bogies, traps and divots.

146. If you can't play tennis, don't despair.
If you can't play, watch tennis live or on TV.
If you can't watch, read about tennis.
If you can't read, dream about tennis.
If you can't dream, okay, try golf!

147. Build a court at your house and they will come!

148. Don't attempt to fulfill your frustrated tennis ambitions through your children.

149. A missed tennis date is a terrible thing to waste.

150. Please! Don't talk about golf on the tennis court.

151. Don't squelch a child's interest in tennis with too much instruction, or too much stress on accuracy or competition.

152. Don't play at segregated clubs or segregated courts.

153. The ideal drop shot bounces twice before reaching the service backline.

154. If at first you don't succeed–serve, rally, volley, lob, drop shot and poach again.

155. Avoid sarcastic looks and remarks toward your opponents. Just give them your best tennis shots.

156. Stick with the basics when things are going wrong.

157. Learn at least one new shot or serve or get to know a new player each tennis season.

*Think About It*

This is the true joy in life,
the being used for a purpose,
recognized by yourself as a mighty one;
the being thoroughly worn out
before you are thrown on the scrap heap;
the being a force of nature
instead of a feverish selfish little clod
of ailments and grievances, complaining
that the world will not devote itself
to making you happy.

—*George Bernard Shaw*

158. Play year-round, inside and out.

159. Among the strongest shots in tennis is the inside-out forehand.

160. Take your racquet on trips both abroad and domestically.

161. Reread your favorite book on tennis.

162. Make new friends through tennis.

163. Eat bananas and other sources of potassium to avoid cramping while at play.

164. Play three person (two-on-one) doubles if the fourth fails to show up.

165. Meet strangers through tennis.

166. Briefly suspend play during the *Star Spangled Banner, Oh Canada, God Save the Queen,* the *Marsellaise, Waltzing Matilda,* earthquakes, funerals and prayers.

167. Golfers like good lies. Ideally about 72 per 18 holes. There are no lies in tennis.

168. It is annoying to your opponents and partners if you can't remember the score. Repeat it aloud frequently.

169. Root for Davis Cup teams.

170. Buy your new house near a tennis center, club, school or park–or with its own court!

171. Support good tennis programs.

172. Good ball-toss is as necessary to effective serving as mustard is to hot-dogs.

173. Stay at hotels and motels with tennis courts and use them.

174. Combine the drop shot with the lob to yo-yo your opponent.

175. On sunny days, wear ultraviolet protective eyewear on the court.

176. When the news is discouraging, turn to tennis.

177. Imagine a good game and you'll play better.

178. Buy good tennis books and instructional materials. However, don't take everything the pros say at face value.

179. Be a hustler on the court; get to everything.

180. Rotate your body to get power in your shots.

181. Play tennis with your children.

182. Don't ask for the score and then dispute the one you are given.

183. Youth and running beat age and cunning.

184. Learn the *Tennis Player's Prayer* and post it in your den.

## Tennis TeNets Top Ten TipsTips–Number 5

GET YOUR RACQUET IN POSITION EARLY. Early racquet preparation is essential to good tennis shots. Get your racquet in position as soon as you can determine whether you'll need a forehand or backhand. You must prepare the racquet while on-the-move and with your eyes on the ball. Think PRE (Position Racquet Early) until it becomes automatic.

185. Have some tennis mementos in your workplace.

186. Use no-ad scoring or play tie-breaks when time is running out.

187. A bad day at court is better than any golf at all.

188. Regarding line calls–unfortunately, some players call them as they need them.

189. See how long you can sustain volleying with a partner as a part of your warm-up.

190. Wear warm-ups to warm up and cool down.

191. Take tennis advice with a grain of salt.

192. Tennis a sissy game? U.S. Tennis Association Rule 31 says you can't suspend play to recover strength or catch your breath!

193. A short game inside service lines is especially good for sharpening your eye-hand coordination, racquet preparation and foot work.

*Think About It*

When we plant a rose seed in the earth, we notice that is it small, but we do not criticize it as "rootless and stemless." We treat it as a seed, giving it the water and nourishment required of a seed. When it first shoots up out of the earth, we don't condemn it as immature and underdeveloped; nor do we criticize the buds for not being open when they appear. We stand in wonder at the process taking place and give the plant the care it needs at each stage of its development. The rose is a rose from the time it is a seed to the time it dies. Within it at all times it contains its whole potential. It seems to be constantly in the process of change; yet at each stage, at each moment, it is perfectly all right as it is."

–W. Timothy Gallwey, *The Inner Game of Tennis,* p. 37
Jonathan Cape Ltd., 32 Bedford Square,
London, WC1B 3EL, ISBN 0 224 01178 2

194. Concentration is a key to good tennis. Note how often one small break in concentration during play can change the entire complexion of a game, set or match.

195. Applaud good shots with the racquet face and one hand.

196. Develop a socially acceptable and unobtrusive way of venting your frustrations.

197. Believe in miracles. You are one!

198. Keep band-aids, aspirin, a quarter for the phone, sunblock, wristlets, sweat bands, a talisman, etc. in your equipment bag. Oh yes! A racquet, balls and *Tennis TeNets: Wit and Wisdom On and Off the Court.*

199. Chris Evert is an excellent role model for any young player.

200. No amount of instruction will improve your game unless you put it into practice, practice, practice.

201. Play so a faulty line call doesn't make the only difference between winning and losing.

202. Improve your tennis performance by improving your attitude toward life.

203. Don't accept "good enough" as good enough for your tennis shots.

204. Laugh at your mistakes; make note of your successes.

205. Keep the wrist firm when volleying.

206. Don’t give back a break of serve.

207. Chances for winners are high if you hit the ball within two feet of your opponents’ baseline.

208. Unforced errors are probably the most frequent cause of losing at tennis.

209. Calm troubled waters for others. Be a peacemaker, but don’t interfere.

## Tennis TeNets Top Ten Tips–Number 6

KEEP MOVING. Keep on the move to meet the ball in time to make good shots. Bend your knees and be ready to move in any direction. Moving forward gives added power to your stroke, a better angle for your shot and less time for your opponent to react and reach the ball. Notice how the pros and good players constantly keep their feet moving even while waiting to return serve.

210. Use cross-court angles to open up the court.

211. Be enthusiastic about the tennis success of others.

212. Give your partner a big high-five for a good shot, point or game.

213. Some say the seventh game is the most important in a set. Actually every game is crucial, but some just seem more crucial than others.

214. The sliced forehand is a very effective, but often neglected shot.

215. One critical successful shot can turn a tennis match into a win.

216. Enhance your image on the court by retrieving balls from the court surface with your racquet. Note how the good players do it.

217. In tennis, it's extra fun to love thy neighbor.

218. One of Rod (Rocket) Laver's favorite instructions to students was "racquet back and give it a whack!"

219. An ace on the golf course puts you in the hole. An ace in tennis can get you out of a hole.

220. It is oversimplified to say that the key to good tennis is practice because if you practice your mistakes, you won't improve.

221. Hit it back and hope.

222. Tennis is not a life or death matter.

223. Put *something* on every shot–topspin, slice, extra pace, off-speed, angle or arc. Go for the baseline, alley or drop-shot, moon shot, lob, dink or smash.

224. There are only a few strokes in tennis–forehand, backhand, serve and volley, but an infinity of shots from these strokes.

225. Don't get overconfident when you're ahead. Play as if the score were reversed.

226. As in baseball, hit 'em where they ain't.

227. Disguise your drop shot. The element of surprise is important to its success.

228. Tennis shoes are not just for the little old lady who owned the used car the dealer wants to sell you. Now, shoes can even include air pumps or lights.

229. To correct your faults, it's better to tell yourself what *to* do rather than what *not to* do.

230. Judge tennis success by how much you enjoy it.

231. Simulate match play as part of your practice.

232. One crucial missed shot can turn a tennis match into a defeat.

233. Aces are a server's best friend.

*Think About It*

## Tennis TeNets Parody

On ***Don't Quit*** (Author Unknown)

*When your strokes go wrong as they sometimes will;*
*When the match you're playing seems all up hill.*
*When your serves fall low and the net seems high;*
*And you charge the net but your volleys fly.*
*With opponents pressing you down a bit—*
*Lob if you must, but don't you quit!*
*Success is failure turned about;*
*A change of pace could bail you out.*
*You never know when you'll get a close call*
*Or opponents will flub an easy ball.*
*Success may be near when it seems afar,*
*So stick to your game when you're hardest hit.*
*It's when things go wrong that you must not quit.*

234. Live by the drop shot–die by the drop shot.

235. Be happy for the net-cord that goes your way. The next may not.

236. Note! You are about to read **the** secret of winning tennis. Hit the ball over the net into the court!

237. To improve your game, compete with yourself as well as your opponents.

238. It's often a good idea to hit to your opponents' backhand.

239. Hit the ball back to your opponents in warm-up but try unobtrusively to do better than they do.

240. Never throw a racquet or bash a ball in anger.

241. Tennis games are won and lost one point at a time. Be patient!

242. Maintain the same routine before every serve.

243. Little or no backswing is needed for volleys.

244. Don't explain your missed shots.

245. Play to win, not to avoid losing.

246. Decide what makes tennis most fun for you and emphasize that.

247. Put a little rosin, like baseball players use, on your racquet handle to improve your grip.

248. Learn to hear the ping that tells you your racquet strings are at the right tension for you.

249. It pays to play with good equipment.

250. Vary your spin.

251. Strategically place your shot when you have time, but above all, get the ball back in the court.

252. You can over-apologize for a bad call or shot.

253. Contrary to what some commercials say, image is not everything in tennis or anything else.

254. Spectators should not be asked to settle disputed line calls.

255. Insist on proper tennis protocol unless it would embarrass the other player(s).

256. Flip a coin or twirl a racquet to determine first-to-serve or court preference.

**Tennis TeNets Top Ten Tips–Number 7**

STEP INTO YOUR SHOT. Stepping into your shot helps you give it accuracy, pace and power. As you step in, you begin moving into the court, enabling you to give your shots greater depth and better direction. Stepping in also helps you hit through the ball and follow through. Watch how the good hitters in tennis and baseball step into the ball.

257. Donate to the National Junior Tennis League. It helps the development of young talent.

258. Don't concede until the last point is over! Remember, as in opera, "It ain't over 'til the fat lady sings."

259. Don't blame the wind or sun unless you're indoors.

260. Win the first point to set yourself up for the rest of the game, tie-break, set or match.

261. Develop backspin.

262. "Out" or "let" calls must be made immediately. Justice delayed is justice denied.

263. Promise "highlights at 10:00" for great shots.

264. Never underestimate the power of a lob (especially when it's short, low and smashed back at a vital part of your anatomy).

265. Balance power with touch and vice versa.

266. Visually project the grid made by the net squares onto the service court area and aim your serves at one of these squares.

267. Big servers have the advantage in tie-breaks.

268. Learn to play doubles well in the deuce or ad court, but feel free to express a preference for where you play best.

269. Don't be suckered into buying gimmicks to improve your game.

*Think About It*

## ***"Take Time"*** (Author Unknown)

*Take time to think,*
*It is the source of power.*
*Take time to play,*
*It is the secret of perpetual youth.*
*Take time to read,*
*It is the fountain of wisdom.*
*Take time to pray,*
*It is the greatest power on earth.*
*Take time to love and be loved,*
*It is a God-given privilege.*
*Take time to be friendly,*
*It is the road to happiness.*
*Take time to laugh,*
*It is the music of the soul.*
*Take time to give,*
*It is too short a day to be selfish.*
*Take time to work,*
*It is the price of success.*

270. The service line is 21 feet from the net. That's the forecourt, from whence you make those great volleys and overhead smashes!

271. Early morning tennis can be beautiful, the more so if you win.

272. In professional tournaments, they introduce new balls after the first seven games and every nine games thereafter. Change yours once in awhile.

273. Pace yourself so you can last three sets.

274. Layer up and don't be afraid to play outdoors in cold, dry weather.

275. Take the initiative to get up a doubles game.

276. Don't play down to weaker opponents–but don't wipe them out either.

277. Good form produces good shots.

278. Always shake hands, say thanks and find something good to say after the match.

279. Mix up your cross-courts with down-the-line shots.

280. Help your instructors by telling them how you learn best.

281. Play unto others as you would have them play unto you.

282. Keep tennis in perspective in your life–after all, it's just a game.

283. Beware! To tennis players, love means nothing.

284. Playing one or more tie-breakers instead of sets is great when remaining time is limited.

285. If your opponents get mad it should say more about them than about you.

286. Take a few lessons now and then.

## Tennis TeNets Top Ten Tips–Number 8

HIT THROUGH THE BALL. Each stroke requires getting the racquet prepared early, hitting *through* (rather than *at*) the ball and letting the racquet give the ball the desired direction, spin and pace. Punch through your volleys too!

287. Most tennis points are lost rather than won.

288. During pregame warm-up, get the balls back to the server so minimum effort is needed to retrieve them. It's not the time to practice your return of serve.

289. Find out if your doubles partner likes to hold two or three balls while serving.

290. To serve well, you must have a consistent toss!

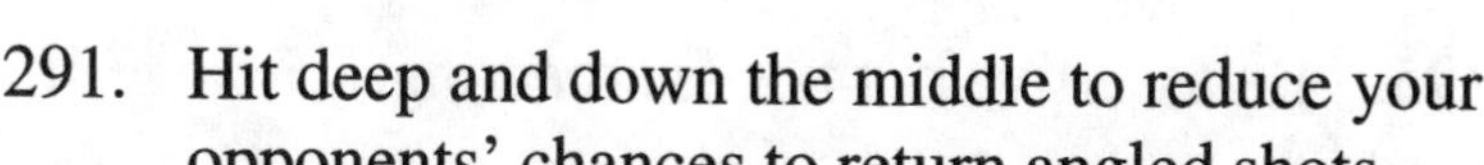

291. Hit deep and down the middle to reduce your opponents' chances to return angled shots.

292. Select your clothes and equipment for fit and comfort so that you are unaware of them during play.

293. While playing, don't interact with non-players or players on adjacent courts.

294. Be religious about your tennis, but don't miss attending your place of worship to play.

295. Be assertive but not overbearing.

296. If they aggravate you so much, why are you still playing with them?

297. Vary the depth as well as the direction of your shots.

298. Remember you play by ear as well as by eye. The ping, ding, thunk or clunk of the ball from your opponent's racquet tells you a lot about the shot that's coming.

299. Apologize, but be happy to win a frame shot. You paid for the whole racquet.

300. Make it fun to be your partner.

301. Help your doubles partner by anticipating an out ball and calling “out” or “bounce it.”

302. Concentrate on the point of contact–where the racquet meets the ball.

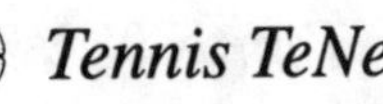



303. A well-placed dink put where they ain't is better than a reachable drive.

304. If your opponents are feeding off your pace, give them some "junk."

305. In doubles, don't let your opponent's egg-on-your-face, down-the-line winner discourage poaching.

306. When in doubt, hit it down the middle as deep as you can (inside the baseline).

307. Stock up on balls on sale. “Penn” them up in your refrigerator to help keep them fresh.

308. Good depth on your shots is more effective if mixed with short stuff.

309. Lobs can be a good offense as well as a good defense. Be a good lobster; it may help you claw your way back into a delicious point.

310. Anticipate the most probable return of serve you can expect.

*Think About It*

There are many who are living far below their possibilities because they are continually handing over their individualities to others. Do you want to be a power in the world? Then be yourself. Be true to the highest within your soul and then allow yourself to be governed by no customs or conventionalities or arbitrary man-made rules that are not founded on principle.

—*Ralph Waldo Emerson*

311. Don't let bad line calls upset your game. Never retaliate with bad calls of your own.

312. A moderately-paced first serve that's in is better than a powerful missed first followed by a patsy second.

313. The angle at which your serve goes over the net is the most likely angle of the return.

314. Be forgiving of yourself and others in tennis as you should in other aspects of your life.

315. To prepare for the upcoming match, study your opponents' warm-up shots and practice serves.

316. Know the playing surface, how it affects your footing and the way the ball bounces.

317. It may be better to take the choice-of-court than be first to serve when weather conditions will influence play.

318. Bud Collins says deuces are the terrible twos.

319. There is no tennis counterpart of the mulligan in golf. That tells you something about the difference between the sports!

320. Never underestimate the value of getting the ball back. Your opponent might make an error.

321. Remember, most rallies probably average fewer than 3.5 exchanges–it must be that .5 exchange that's critical!

322. Learn to volley effectively. The volley deprives your opponents of time to make good returns.

323. Should-a, would-a, could-a and might-have-beens–block them out of your mind.

324. Use a ball machine and bang board. But nothing beats real play, practice and instruction.

325. Take more chances at 40-love and 40-15 or love-40 and 15-40.

326. Do your personal best on each point; the game, set and match will take care of themselves.

327. An ace on the court is worth two up your sleeve.

328. Be a human backboard. Hit everything back!

329. Be generous with offering "take-two serves" when play is interrupted.

330. Tennis players love to be courted.

331. Build your game eclectically–take good elements from various good players.

332. Watch yourself play on videotape at least once. You'll be surprised, but don't let it discourage you.

333. Teach someone else; it helps your game too!

334. Don't plant your feet at the net. Move with the anticipated direction of the ball.

## Tennis TeNets Top Ten Tips–Number 9

FOLLOW THROUGH. Complete your shot by continuing your racquet, arm and body motion after you hit through the ball to get accuracy, power and good depth or placement. Your shot is not complete until you have followed through. Following through also helps you get into position for your next shot.

335. Take care of small injuries so they don't get worse.

336. Get your rotator cuff repaired, your hip replaced or arthroscopic surgery for your knee–anything to keep on playing.

337. Call "Mine!" for shots you want in doubles.

338. Ice down your injuries as soon as possible.

339. If at first you don't succeed, serve again.

340. Strive for accuracy, then power.

341. Have a good, but modest, equipment bag.

342. Tennis players never want to give the other guy a break–service break, that is.

343. Weak players blame their equipment.

344. The wind, the sun and adverse court conditions are on the side of the able tennis player.

345. Don't be sexist about your tennis, especially in mixed doubles.

346. Tennis players often beat themselves.

347. Find good balls at bargain prices and share them liberally.

348. Play with style but without pretension.

349. Make sure your feet are moving, especially when receiving serve.

*Think About It*

***Learn as if you are going to live and play tennis forever!***

350. Instead of aiming right at the line or corner, aim with a margin of safety as the pros do.

351. Don't let the "KILL" impulse ruin your smash.

352. Don't take a long break from tennis. Shots and skills get rusty fast.

353. Use proper exercise to prevent tennis elbow. It's difficult to cure.

354. Use sunscreen and wear a visor or tennis hat.

355. The greatest tennis match of all time is yet to be played.

356. Poaching is fine for tennis and eggs, but not for hunting or fishing.

357. Talk with friends and family about tennis, but don't blow your own horn.

358. Tennis brings out the best and worst in players' personalities. It rarely transforms them.

**Tennis TeNets Top Ten Tips–Number 10**

CONCENTRATE. Keep your mind on the point you are playing at the present moment. Focus only on the shot and point in the here and now. Try for deep concentration in which you are oblivious to everything else. Tennis games are won one point at a time. A wandering mind gathers few points!

359. Have a standard routine to receive and return serves. It's just as important as a regular routine before serving.

360. Never quit before the match is finished except by mutual consent.

361. Concentrate on the point of contact–where the racquet meets the ball.

362. Maintaining balance is important and bending your knees is a key to good balance.

363. Remember, you own half the court.

364. Complement and compliment your doubles partner. This is especially important if you are playing with your spouse or significant other!

365. Plan your serve and point development while you are retrieving the balls and preparing to serve.

366. On some service returns, chip the return and charge the net, daring the server to pass you.

367. Physical fitness is necessary for good tennis. Good tennis helps keep you physically fit.

368. An asset of your game is to have a "good eye"–knowing when a ball is going out and letting it go.

369. If you are having difficulty returning serve, try standing very close to the service baseline to half-volley your return. It may rattle the server into loss of concentration or faults.

370. The objective of the return-of-serve is either to win the point or put the ball in play.

371. Some say singles is a game of patience while doubles is a game of controlled aggression.

372. Remember, down-the-line shots have to clear the net six inches higher than cross-courts over the middle of the net.

373. Stay aggressive; keep going forward and finish the point.

374. Take the ball on the rise whenever possible.

375. When things are going well with your game, it's best not to analyze it or focus on its elements.

376. In serve and volley tennis, matches may consist primarily of who serves best, who returns best and who gets to the net first.

377. Don't take time to admire your shots; keep moving!

378. Compliment good shots. The code of silence prevails about bad ones.

379. The lob is not a sissy shot. You can become a good "lobbyist."

380. Most breaks of serve follow a break of serve; thus the breaker becomes the breakee.

381. In doubles, good approach shots go down the middle, low over the net and deep in the court.

382. Get the racquet back as soon as you see if the ball is coming to your forehand or backhand.

383. Today is the first day of the rest of your tennis life–don't waste it.

384. Volley with the ball well out in front of you, a stiff wrist and the racquet head up.

385. Take the ball early, in the air or on the rise. It gives your opponent less time to return your shot.

*Think About It*

Visit Wimbledon, the site of the All England Lawn Tennis Championships. There is a great museum with informative exhibits and a fine library. Rudyard Kipling's famous lines from "If" are inscribed over the player's entrance to Centre Court.

*"If you can meet with triumph and disaster*
*And treat those two impostors just the same.*
*Yours is the Earth and everything that's in it . . ."*

Other lines from "If" are equally apt for tennis players.

*"If you can keep your head when all about you*
*are losing theirs and blaming it on you,*
*If you can trust yourself when all men doubt you,*
*But make allowance for their doubting too . . ."*

386. While waiting around the court, learn to bounce the ball with the rim of your racquet perpendicular to the court. It's surprisingly easy and good for eye-hand coordination.

387. Good racquet preparation means more than just getting the racquet back.

388. Always announce the score. Tennis players have good memories, but they are short (their memories, that is).

389. Practice top spin lobs and the overheads required to defend against them.

390. The seams on the ball are there for aerodynamics. They help the ball go straight or, through spin, to curve and drop. Learn to *read* the spin on the ball so you can anticipate its bounce.

391. Too many compliments cheapen them. Be generous but honest with your compliments.

392. Read your opponents' court position and body language to help you decide how to play the next point.

393. Practice your stroke motions while watching tennis on TV.

394. You need mental toughness for tennis and for life's big and little problems.

395. Be sure to win the deuce point; it gives you the advantage.

396. If you win the ad point, you've won the game or two more chances to stay in it.

397. Consistency is the name of the game in tennis.

398. Every tennis match should end with a handshake and the exchange of compliments and pleasantries.

399. Listen to what your opponents are saying to themselves and exploit the attitude reflected.

400. Look, act and behave as if you were a better tennis player and you are more likely to become one.

401. You may not get rich in tennis but you could have a net gain in a rally.

402. Don't get caught in "no-man's land," the area around the service back line.

403. The best alibi in tennis doubles? "Yours!"

404. In doubles, select a strategy for deciding how balls down the middle will be handled.

405. Don't tense up on set point.

406. It's not fair to foot-fault, although its often easy to get away with.

407. You don't have to sue to take a friend to court.

408. The ball is moving, the court is not. Keep your eye on the ball.

## Tennis TeNets Top Ten Tips–PLUS ONE

**ENJOY!** Tennis is a game! Games should be fun and enjoyable. In addition to the joy it can bring you, tennis can help keep you physically and mentally healthy. It can improve the quality and length of your life. Don't spoil the fun by trying too hard, losing your temper or injuring yourself. The happier you are in playing, the more joy you'll give to others and yourself. Enjoy!

409. Tennis champions kiss trophies.

410. Graciously retrieve and return errant balls from adjacent courts.

411. Who can resist trying to steer a wide shot into the court with body contortions?

412. To get away early and discreetly from work for tennis just say, "I'm expected at court."

413. Tennis players have their faults.

414. Learn to live with an inexplicable fact of life–one day you'll play great, the next day not!

415. Relaxed concentration is a key to good tennis.

416. Don't encroach on an adjacent court in play to retrieve your ball.

417. Don't overspend your budget on tennis.

418. Try to have a consistent contact point for meeting the ball with your racquet.

419. Create more ways to have more fun while playing tennis.

420. What a satisfying shot, the overhead smash! How frustrating to blow it!

421. Exploit the pace of your opponents' shots.

422. Good wrist snap delivers more power to the serve.

423. Get to the ball early (the tennis ball, not the dance).

424. Someone said, "If tennis were a religion, Wimbledon would be its temple."

425. You learn much about yourself and others through playing tennis.

426. Punch your volleys.

427. If you follow a weak shot to the net, you may get passed or lobbed.

428. Don't let tennis interfere with your career. Don't let your career interfere with tennis.

*Think About It*

It is not the critic who counts. The credit belongs to the man who is actually in the arena . . . who at the best knows in the end the triumphs of high achievements and who at the worst, if he fails, at least fails while daring greatly, so that his place will never be with those cold and timid souls who know neither victory or defeat.

—*Theodore Roosevelt*

429. The best time for a double fault is when your opponent is serving.

430. Swing through your ground strokes.

431. Dictate play. Be the aggressor!

432. Learn the two-handed backhand if you can.

433. Follow a deep approach shot to the net.

434. Think of the racquet as if it was an extension of your arm and hand.

435. Take small steps rather than big strides to get into position.

436. Drop shots are risky when tried from deep in the court or behind the baseline.

437. It's better to be good *and* lucky rather than either just good *or* lucky.

438. It's a good idea to spin in your second serve; it won't make you a confirmed "spinster."

439. Tennis players love backhand compliments.

440. Play consistent tennis and wait for your opponent to make the errors. But go for it when your chance comes.

441. Whether you win or lose the first set, play the second as if you were starting anew.

442. Contribute to a tennis scholarship at your alma mater.

443. Don't get mad or get even, get ahead!

444. Be consistent. Variation in stroke production causes errors.

445. Tennis players have great legs! Tennis develops them!

446. Cover the whole court, but don't hog it in doubles.

447. Overcome *egalité* when playing a French opponent.

*Think About It*

*The optimist says 50% of all tennis players win!*
*The pessimist says 50% of all tennis players lose!*
*The realist says anyone who plays tennis is a winner!*

448. Some tennis points are psychological.

449. A service winner is as good as an ace.

450. Talk with your doubles partner frequently regarding poaching, court coverage, strategies and maneuvers.

451. Commentators' tips? Easy for them to say!

452. Occasionally run around your backhand to hit an inside-out forehand.

453. Don't let them discover that your backhand is weak.

454. Stay low on the forehand drive.

455. Use wit to make tennis more fun, but remember, you can be too witty.

456. Make your racquet play string music.

457. As you work to improve elements of your game, keep in mind the importance of maintaining perspective on your game as a whole.

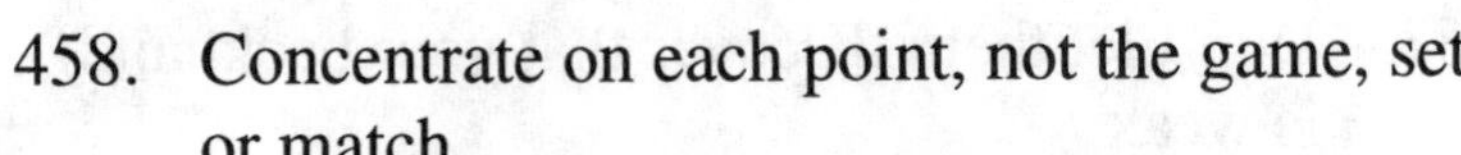

458. Concentrate on each point, not the game, set or match.

459. Cover the net as if you were a soccer or hockey goalkeeper.

460. When things get tense or tough, take a walk around the baseline, take deep breaths, and remind yourself it's just a game.

461. It's difficult to diagnose your own problems or faults. Get help from a pro; the pros do.

**Tennis TeNets Top Ten Tips +1**

1. Watch the ball!
2. Bend your knees!
3. Anticipate, prepare!
4. Rotate your body!
5. Position racquet early!
6. Keep moving!
7. Step into your shot!
8. Hit through the ball!
9. Follow through!
10. Concentrate!

+1 ENJOY!

462. Set up early and correctly for the particular shot you expect to make.

463. Exploit top spin.

464. You've got to play the game that's best for you. Change your game only as a last resort.

465. Check the bounceability of your tennis balls. They should rebound as high as the net-cord.

466. Golfers get "teed off."

467. Like tennis players, some ministers make double faults in Sunday morning services–too weak and too long.

468. Try to remember the points in your games. Note how the pros remember every shot.

469. Cool down! Both ways!!

470. Make your coach happy–win!

471. Bring joy and laughter to the court.

472. A tennis player can be a friend of the court.

473. Players who apologize may gloat a little in secret when they win points on net-cords, woodies or miss-hits.

474. Read Bud Collins' *Modern Encyclopedia of Tennis.*

475. Move your opponents up and back as well as from side to side to keep them off balance.

476. Major changes in the way you play may cause you to lose for a while. Hang in there.

477. The racquet's sweet spot is the area on its face (the strings) that gives the most accuracy and power to your shots. On good days, it's of adequate size; other days you can't even find it.

478. Cultivate an image of yourself as a successful and happy tennis player.

479. Attend matches of your friends and relatives and cheer them on.

480. Concentrate on the point of the moment. Shut out distractions and competing thoughts.

481. Patience! Winning a tennis point means getting the ball over the net and into the court only one time more than your opponents.

482. Don't pause to admire your shots; the return may come back out-of-reach.

483. The derivation of the word tennis may be from the Latin, *tenére*, to hold.

484. Support worthy sponsorship and beneficiaries of tennis tournaments.

485. In trying to improve your game, look for progress, not perfection.

486. The ad court seems to draw more service double faults than the deuce court.

487. It's very tempting but may be disastrous to get overconfident if you easily win the first few games.

488. The old tennis player said, "I've served under seven U.S. Presidents."

489. If you see you are going to lose, go down swinging and learn from the experience.

490. Enjoy friends' tennis experiences and share yours without always having to top theirs.

491. In doubles, both players should be at net or both back unless special strategy dictates otherwise, for example, for a big serving opponent.

492. Good eye-hand coordination is essential to tennis. Improved eye-hand coordination can be developed with effective exercise and practice.

493. It's demoralizing to lose a game after being ahead 40-love. Try to make this happen to your opponents.

494. A miniature game of tennis, played in the area bounded by the service lines, is a good warm-up and excellent practice.

495. Tennis is nonsexist. All rules apply equally to both sexes. Exceptions are the length of tournament matches: 3 sets for women, with a break between 2 and 3; 5 sets for men.

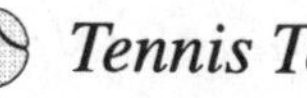


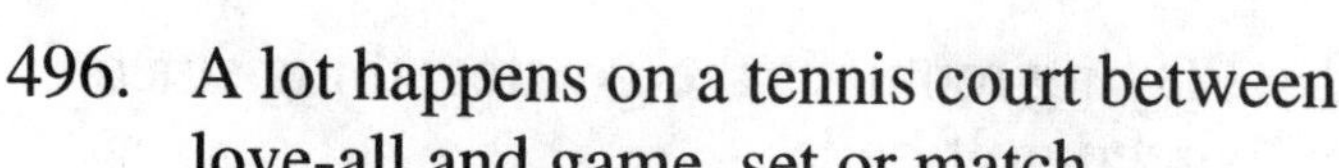

496. A lot happens on a tennis court between love-all and game, set or match.

497. Enjoy tennis and share *Tennis TeNets* with a friend.

498. Sphairistike is the ancient name for tennis. Using it probably won't impress anyone, even your friends.

499. Practice, practice, practice. Play, play, play. Enjoy, enjoy, enjoy.

500. Playing tennis is the greatest thing since sliced golf balls.

501. Don’t leave your best game and good behavior on the practice court.

502. Look for tennis humor and pass it along.

503. Think about how the great game of tennis can enrich your life and the lives of others and make it happen.

504. Share your own tennis tenets.

505. Tennis is mentioned in the Bible second only to baseball. For baseball it says, "In the big inning." For tennis it says, "Ruth served in the court of Boaz." No known reference is made to golf.

506. Maybe the family that plays together stays together. It's worth the effort.

507. Tennis and the good life require lifelong learning. Be a lifelong learner of both games.

508. Remember that every game, set or match begins with the score at love-all!

## *Tennis Player's Prayer*

Dear Lord, please let me hit the ball
so well that even I,
When telling of it afterward
will never need to lie.

And make my ground-stroke straight
and true.
My backhand swift and firm.
And help me with a serve that makes
my opposition squirm.

Protect me from the double fault.
Assist me at the net.
Endow me with an overhead
that travels like a jet.

Above all, Lord, this pleasure
is a thing I'd like to share.
So when you grant my wish be sure
that all my friends are there!

*—Author Unknown*